Penguins, Penguins, Everywhere!

To Al Beck,
a wonderful teacher,
mentor, and friend
who helped me unleash
my inner penguin
many years ago.

Special thanks to Paul Erickson,
formerly of the New England Aquarium,
who graciously shared his knowledge
of these fascinating little creatures.

ISBN-13: 978-0-545-00086-4
ISBN-10: 0-545-00086-6

25   19 20 21 22 23 24/0

Printed in the U.S.A.   40

First Scholastic printing, February 2007

Book design by Sara Gillingham and Katie Jennings
Typeset in Softie
The illustrations in this book were rendered in cut and torn paper.

Penguins, Penguins, Everywhere!

By Bob Barner

SCHOLASTIC INC.

New York Toronto London Auckland Sydney
Mexico City New Delhi Hong Kong Buenos Aires

Some penguins live in icy places.

and some live in the heat.

Their colors help them hid

when they fish for fishy treats.

Cold penguins huddle close

with penguin heat to share.

Daddies warm warm fragile eggs

with tender, special care.

Hot penguins fluff their feathers

to cool off from the sun.

Their chicks call out from shady

caves to ask for food and fun.

Noisy penguins waddle

and toboggan to the sea.

Each one honks to find

its mate wherever it may be.

Penguins watch for sneaky seals.

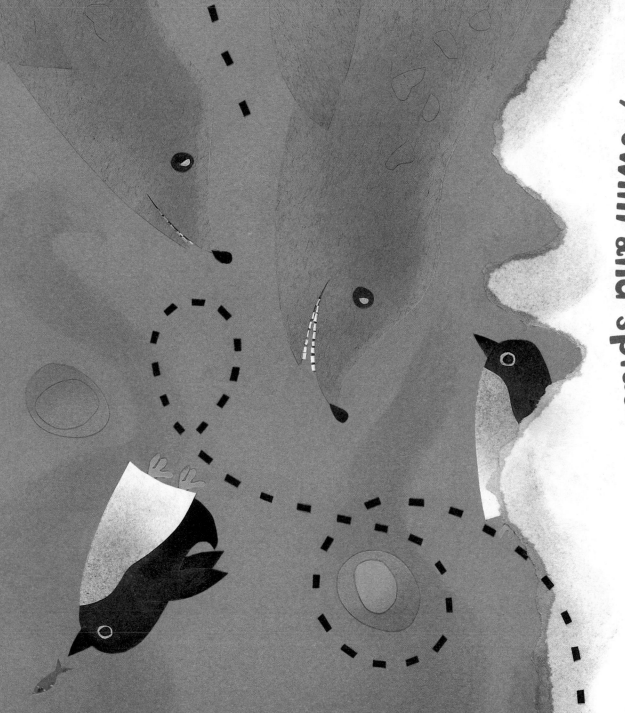

as they swim and splash and play.

Sleepy little penguins end

another perfect day.

How do penguins move?

Tiptoe

Waddle

Dive

Gulls

Snakes

Seals

Orcas

Why do penguins look the way they do?

In the water, black feathers blend in with the ocean bottom. This makes it hard for hungry penguin eaters to see the penguins from above.

White feathers blend in with the light colored sky so hungry penguin eaters can't spot penguins from below.

Penguin Parade

Chinstrap
South Sandwich Islands

24 inches
10 pounds

Emperor
Antarctica

45 inches
90 pounds

Black-Footed
Also called "African Penguin"
Africa

20 inches
6½ pounds

Erect-Crested
Islands off the coast
of New Zealand

20 inches
8 pounds

Magellanic
Argentina

26 inches
11 pounds

Yellow-Eyed
New Zealand

30 inches
11 pounds

Fiordland
New Zealand

23 inches
6½ pounds

Gentoo
Falkland Islands

22 inches
13 pounds

King
South Georgia Island

28 inches
30 pounds

Galápagos
Galápagos Islands

20 inches
5 pounds

Rockhopper
South America

16 inches
5 pounds

Humboldt
Peru

25 inches
9 pounds

Snares Island
Snares Island

16 inches
6½ pounds

Adélie
Antarctica

24 inches
9 pounds

Macaroni
Falkland Islands

28 inches
9½ pounds

Royal
Macquarie Island

27 inches
10 pounds

Little Blue
Also called "Fairy Penguin"
New Zealand

16 inches
2½ pounds